Paleo

30 Days of

MW01098301

By: Mary Scott

Introduction

Paleo breakfasts are almost reason alone to switch to the Paleo lifestyle as the choices are delicious and they all pack an energy punch. However, it is easy to get into an egg and bacon rut which can lead to cravings for those old days of carb-filled breads and sugary treats. This book lays out 30 days' worth of breakfast options that will help you get out of the old brekkie box and enjoy the full potential of a Paleo lifestyle.

Try Banana Chocolate Almond Crepes or Artichoke Eggwiches, maybe whip up some Sweet Potato and Red Pepper Cups for the weekend or start the day off right with a quick and delicious Orange Vanilla Smoothie.

The way you start your day sets the tone for the next 24 hours, which means breakfast is really the most important meal of the day and making it a healthy and nutritious one is important. So start your 30 day adventure of Paleo deliciousness and get ready to fall in love with breakfast all over again.

Wishing you Paleo Health!

Mary

Disclaimer

Table of Contents

Breakfast Recipes

Eggs in Red Pepper and Sweet Potato Cups

Serves: 4
Prep Time: 15 min.
These little red and orange cups pack a big flavor punch and look pretty cute to boot. The bright orange color of the sweet potatoes signals their nutrient superiority over the standard breakfast potato. The sweet potato is coupled with the protein power of eggs for a breakfast of champions.

Ingredients
2 sweet potatoes, cooked
2 red bell pepper, diced
8 eggs
1/4 cup coconut milk
1 tsp salt
1 tsp paprika
Coconut oil

Directions
1. Preheat oven to 350 degrees and lightly coat a 12-cup muffin tin with coconut oil.
2. Mash the sweet potatoes and mix in red bell pepper, 1 tbsp. coconut oil and a 1/2 tsp of salt.
3. Press approximately 1 tablespoon of mixture into each tin as to form little cups and stick in the oven for 30 minutes.
4. Mix together eggs and coconut milk.
5. Heat coconut oil in nonstick pan over medium heat and add eggs, stir until cooked.
6. Spoon eggs into potato cups and serve.

Nutrition
Calories 191
Carbs 14
Fat 10
Protein 13
Sodium 270
Sugar 5

Paleo Breakfast Chili and Eggs

Serves: 4 - 6
Prep Time: 20 min.

Bring on the Mexican flavor for a brand new twist to the morning. A breakfast chili topped with eggs provides a ton of protein and gives not only makes for a great flavor boost but also a big kick of energy for your busy morning.

Ingredients
1/2 pound ground beef
1 medium-sized onion, chopped
1 celery stalk, diced
2 tomatoes, diced
1/2 cup water
4 cloves garlic, minced
Taco seasoning
8 eggs
Salt and pepper to taste

Directions
1. Over medium heat, brown ground beef, onions, garlic and celery.
2. Stir in tomato and taco seasoning and half cup of water and cook for 5 minutes on low.
3. Break eggs into chili skillet and cover for 5 minutes.

Nutrition
Calories 242
Carbs 10
Fat 13
Protein 30
Sodium 141
Sugar 4

Ham and Egg Lettuce Wrap

Serves: 2
Prep Time: 10 min.

Lettuce makes for a handy wrap as the flavor is quite neutral allowing foods rolled up in one to shine. Ham and eggs rolled up in lettuce is a sturdy simple breakfast that can be enjoyed at the table or on-the-go making it versatile for any day of the week.

Ingredients
4 eggs, hard-boiled
4 slices turkey ham
4 iceberg lettuce leaves, large
Salt and pepper to taste

Direction
1. Use 2 lettuce slices per wrap.
2. Slice eggs and place two per wrap.
3. Top with 2 slices turkey ham and roll up.

Nutrition
Calories 180
Carbs 1
Fat 14
Protein 12
Sodium 380
Sugar 1

Spinach Quiche

Serves: 4
Prep Time: 15 min.

Spinach is a super food and in turn a little bit of Popeye iron is a great way to get going in the morning. The slow cooker method also saves tons of time as you don't have to go through the whole creating and waiting process in the morning.

Ingredients
5 cups spinach, washed and chopped
1 small onion, diced
1 tomato, diced
2 cloves garlic, minced
2 tbsp. almond flour
8 eggs
Salt and pepper to taste

Directions
1. Lightly coat medium slow cooker with extra virgin olive oil.
2. In a large mixing bowl, whisk eggs, add tomato and onion and mix.
3. Layer spinach on bottom of slow cooker and pour egg mixture over top.
4. Cook on low for 6 hours.

Nutrition
Calories 215
Carbs 3
Fat 18
Protein 16
Sodium 385
Sugar 1

BLT Wraps

Serves: 4
Prep Time: 20 min.

Ingredients
Wrap
6 eggs
8 tbsp. almond flour
1 tbsp. water
1 tbsp. extra virgin olive oil

Filling
8 slices turkey bacon
2 cups lettuce, washed and dried
2 large tomatoes, sliced

Directions
1. Preheat oven to 350 degrees and place bacon on baking tray.
2. Stick bacon in oven and cook as per instructions.
3. Crack open eggs into large mixing bowl and whisk, add water and flour.
4. Heat 1 tbsp. extra virgin olive oil in medium-sized pan and pour batter until surface of pan is covered, after two minutes, flip tortilla and cook for another moment or so.
5. Allow tortillas to cool and top with bacon, lettuce and tomato.

Nutrition
Calories 265
Carbs 6
Fat 22
Protein 16
Sodium 398
Sugar 2

Open-faced Artichoke Eggwich

Serves: 4
Prep Time: 10 min.

Artichoke hearts are the exact size of egg muffins and are the perfect cradle for breakfast eggs. The vinegar-soak softens up the hearts while giving them a perky flavor.

Ingredients
4 artichoke hearts
4 eggs
1/2 cup apple cider vinegar
Extra virgin olive oil
Salt and pepper

Directions
1. Soak artichoke hearts in vinegar for half hour.
2. Preheat oven at 375 degrees.
3. Place aluminum foil on baking sheet and lightly coat with less than a tsp of extra virgin olive oil.
4. Place artichoke hearts on tray and crack one egg into each heart.
5. Stick in oven for 20 minutes.
6. Enjoy.

Nutrition
Calories 173
Carbs 7
Fat 10
Protein 14
Sodium 600
Sugar 0

Zucchini Maple Sausage

Serves: 4
Prep Time: 20 min.

Ingredients
4 zucchinis
2 extra lean Italian turkey sausage, chopped
1 onion, diced
1 tomato
2 tsp maple syrup
Extra virgin olive oil

Direction
1. Preheat oven to 400 degrees and lightly coat baking tray with extra virgin olive oil.
2. In a non-stick pan, cook sausage and onion over medium heat.
3. Slice zucchini in half vertically and scoop out a little bit of the zucchini meat so you have tunnels.
4. Add zucchini meat and chopped tomatoes into sausage and cook for 5 minutes.
5. Scoop sausage mixture into zucchini, drizzle with maple syrup and bake in oven for 20 minutes.

Nutrition
Calories 220
Carbs 17
Fat 5
Protein 20
Sodium 640
Sugar 8

Prosciutto and Eggplant Sandwiches

Serves: 2
Prep Time: 10 min.

Eggplant has a relatively neutral flavor which makes it a great base for a sandwich and also just as portable. This particular sammy is great for both breakfast and lunch. A sprinkling of flax seed is good for breakfast as it gives your brain an essential amino acid kick start.

Ingredients
2 eggplants
8 slices extra lean prosciutto ham
1/2 avocado, pitted and mashed
1 green bell pepper, sliced
1/2 small onion, peeled and sliced

Directions
1. Preheat oven to 375 degrees.
2. Slice eggplant in half vertically.
3. Spread avocado on one half of each avocado.
4. Next layer place prosciutto, green bell pepper and onions.
5. Wrap each sandwich in aluminum foil and place in oven for 20 minutes.

Nutrition
Calories 108
Carbs 3
Fat 6
Protein 9
Sodium 500
Sugar 1

Chocolate Banana Crepes

Serves: 4

These chocolate banana crepes are a bit of a treat as the Choco-banana goodness does come with some sugar and carbs. However, if you've been sticking with your Paleo plan you can surely sneak in a little sweet to award yourself on the weekend. The great thing with these crepes is you get the chocolate flavor from the cocoa powder which also happens to be very good for you and the walnuts and flaxseed get you some of that good fat.

Crepes
6 eggs
8 tbsp. almond flour
1 tbsp. water
1 tbsp. coconut oil
1 tbsp. cocoa

Filling
3 bananas, sliced into discs
¼ cup chopped walnuts
4 tsp flaxseed
1 tbsp. maple syrup

Directions
1. Crack open eggs into large mixing bowl and whisk, add water and flour.
2. Heat 1 tbsp. coconut oil in medium-sized pan and pour batter until surface of pan is covered and cook for two minutes.
3. Flip tortilla and cook for another moment or so. Set aside.
4. In a bowl, mix together filling ingredients.
5. Scoop filling into crepes and serve.

Nutrition
Calories 324
Carbs 29
Fat 19
Protein 14
Sodium 99
Sugar 15

Overnight Sausage and Sweet Potatoes

Serves: 4
Prep Time: 10 min.

Waking up to comfy prepared breakfast is always great and thanks to the handy slow cooker you can do just that. Sweet potatoes and sausage make for hearty fare and is perfect for winter mornings.

Ingredients

3 lean Italian sausages, chopped
2 sweet potatoes, chopped
2 red bell peppers, diced
1 medium red onion, diced
Salt and pepper to taste

Direction
1. Lightly coat medium-sized slow cooker with extra virgin olive oil and place chopped sweet potatoes on bottom.
2. Place sausage on top so juice will drip into potatoes and then layer pepper and onions.
3. Turn slow cooker on low and allow to cook for 8 hours.

Nutrition
Calories 414
Carbs 25
Fat 25
Protein 23
Sodium 1176
Sugar 3

Basil and Avocado Scrambled Eggs with Zucchini 'Toast'

Serves: 4
Prep Time: 15 min

Ingredients
8 eggs
1/4 cup fresh basil
1 avocado, peeled, pitted and sliced
1/4 cup coconut milk
2 zucchinis, vertically sliced into four pieces
Salt and pepper to taste
Extra virgin olive oil

Directions
1. Preheat oven to 375 degrees and lightly coat cookie sheet with extra virgin olive oil.
2. Place zucchini slices on tray and stick into oven for 15 minutes.
3. Crack eggs into medium mixing bowl and whisk with coconut milk, salt and pepper.
4. Heat 1 tbsp. extra virgin olive oil in skillet and cook eggs over medium heat, adding basil and avocado after a minute of cooking.
5. Remove zucchini "toast" and serve with scrambled eggs.

Nutrition
Calories 203
Carbs 6
Fat 16
Protein 12
Sodium 130
Sugar 0

Daikon Hash Brown

Serves: 2
Prep Time: 10 min.

There is something about cooked daikon that has a fried hash brown kind of flavor and also taken on a hash brown consistency when cooked. The vegetable is a great source of vitamin C amongst other health benefits, making it a healthy substitute for potatoes. This serves 2 as a whole breakfast or 4 as a side dish.

Ingredients
4 cups shredded daikon (white radish)
3 eggs
1 tbsp. almond flour
1 small onion, minced
1 tsp salt
1 tsp black pepper
Extra virgin olive oil

Directions
1. Combine all ingredients except for olive oil in mixing bowl.
2. Heat olive oil in skillet over medium heat and place 2 tbsp. of daikon into skillet, flattening so it resembles a hash brown, and repeat with remainder of daikon.
3. Cook for 5 minutes and then flip and cook for another 5 minutes.

Nutrition
Calories 193
Carbs 10
Fat12
Protein 9
Sodium 154
Sugar 0

Turkey Ham on Portabella

Serves: 2
Prep Time: 10 min.

Ingredients
4 Portabella Mushrooms
4 slices turkey ham, diced
1 egg white
1 red bell pepper
1 lemon juiced
½ tsp salt
Extra virgin olive oil

Directions
1. Preheat oven to 375 degrees and lightly coat baking tray with olive oil.
2. Mix together lemon juice, 1 tbsp. olive oil, salt and bell pepper.
3. Place mushrooms on baking tray and brush with egg white.
4. Lay slice of ham on each heart and top with bell pepper mixture and place in oven for 20 minutes.

Nutrition
Calories 103
Carbs 4
Fat 3
Protein 7
Sodium 84
Sugar 2

Smoked Salmon, Egg and Steamed Artichoke Cups

Serves 4
Prep Time: 10 min.

Salmon is great for your body and brain at any time of the day so a breakfast kick off with this pink gold is a sign of a good day ahead. The artichoke acts as a perfect complement and carrier for the fish.

Ingredients
4 artichoke hearts
4 slices smoked salmon
4 eggs
Salt and pepper to taste

Directions
1. Place artichoke hearts in steamer and steam for 25 minutes.
2. Poach eggs in water for 5 minutes.
3. Remove artichokes from steamer, top with one poached egg and smoked salmon slice.

Nutrition
Calories 175
Carbs 16
Fat 5
Protein 22
Sodium 290
Sugar 2

Deconstructed Egg Salad

Serves: 2
Prep Time: 10 min.

Ingredients
4 eggs, boiled
2 tsp Paleo Mayo (recipe below)
1 tsp fresh dill
1 stalk celery, chopped
1 tomato, chopped
1 cup chopped cucumber
1 cup romaine lettuce, washed and dried

Paleo Mayo
2 eggs
1 3/4 cup extra virgin olive oil
¼ cup lemon juice
1/2 tsp mustard

Directions

Paleo Mayo
1. Place egg yolks and whites in glass bowl and add remaining ingredients.
2. Blend mayo using immersion blender, it should double in size by the time you are finished.

Salad
1. Coarsely chop eggs and add mix with Paleo mayo, dill, salt and pepper.
2. Combine remaining ingredients and serve with scoop of egg atop.

Nutrition
Calories 225
Carbs 2

Fat 10
Protein 31
Sodium 350
Sugar 1

Italian Turkey Sausage and Pepper Toss

Serves: 4
Prep Time: 10 min.

Turkey sausage provides great flavor but with far less fat than traditional pork sausage. This Italian-style toss up complete with bell pepper and zucchini makes for a heart start to the day.

Ingredients
2 extra-lean Italian turkey sausages
1 medium-sized onion
2 green bell peppers
2 zucchinis
Salt and pepper to taste

Directions
1. Place 1 tsp of extra virgin olive oil in skillet over medium heat.
2. Chop turkey sausage into 1/2 inch circles and place in skillet over medium-heat and sauté.
2. Add onions, pepper and zucchini, continuing to sauté until veggies are cooked tender.

Nutrition
Calories 180
Carbs 14
Fat 5
Protein 20
Sodium 640
Sugar 2

Salmon and Arugula Power Salad

Serves: 2
Prep Time: 10 min.

If there is such a thing as a perfect food - the platinum standard of body fuel - then it would be salmon. Start your day off with salmon and you will feel the difference as the essential amino acids cross the brain barrier and give you a boost. This salad is chock full of stuff that provides a full load of energy right through to a late lunch.

Ingredients
2 cans salmon
1/4 cup sunflower seeds
1/4 cup cranberries
1 cup arugula
1 tbsp. extra virgin olive oil
1 tbsp. apple cider vinegar
Salt and pepper to taste

Directions
1. Place salmon in large bowl and mix with olive oil and vinegar.
2. Add remaining ingredients and mix.

Nutrients
Calories 236
Carbs 16
Fat 8
Protein 25
Sodium 380
Sugar 10

Paleo Zucchini, Bacon and Egg Bundles

Serves: 4 - 6
Prep Time: 10 min.

Bacon and eggs are a totally Paleo way to start your day and when you use Turkey bacon you can feel even better about it. In this recipe we give bacon 'n eggs some zucchini packaging so you can enjoy your little protein bomb on-the-go.

Ingredients
12 eggs
12 turkey bacon slices
3 zucchinis, peeled
2 tomatoes
Salt and pepper to taste

Directions
1. Preheat oven to 375 degrees and brush standard muffin tin with extra virgin olive oil.
2. Thinly slice zucchinis vertically so you have 2 x 6 pliable strips.
3. Place three zucchini strips and one bacon strip in each cup so that their centers overlap in the bottom of each tin and you have six zucchini ends and two bacon ends hanging outside of the tin.
4. Crack one egg into each cup and wrap zucchini and bacon over the egg and bake in oven for 25 minutes.

Nutrition (2 per)
Calories 226
Carbs 6
Fat16
Protein 17
Sodium 440
Sugar 2

Portobello Mushroom, Bacon and Eggs

Serves: 2-4
Prep Time: 20 min.

Mushrooms make for a lovely meaty addition to any breakfast plate. Here the robust portabella is topped with enough protein to have you cartwheeling your way through the morning. Enjoy with sliced tomatoes on the side for a palate balance.

Ingredients
4 portabella mushrooms
4 slices turkey bacon
4 eggs
Extra virgin olive oil
Salt and pepper to taste

Directions
1. Preheat oven to 375 degrees and lightly coat baking tray with extra virgin olive oil.
2. Place mushrooms on tray and sprinkle with a little salt and pepper.
3. Crack one egg into each mushroom and lay one bacon slice atop.
4. Bake in oven for 20 minutes.

Nutrition
Calories 131
Carbs 5
Fat 9
Protein 11
Sodium 223
Sugar 0

Smoothies

Strawberry Vanilla Smoothie
Serves: 2
Prep Time: 5 min.

Strawberries are toward the lower end when it comes to sugar content which makes them a great choice for smoothies. The sweetness that they do contain means you don't need to add additional sugar and the almonds give some added protein as well as fat to round out the flavor. Combine all of that with vanilla almond milk and you have yourself a pretty great way to start the day.

Ingredients
1/2 cup strawberries
8 almonds
2 tsp flaxseed
3/4 cup unsweetened vanilla almond milk
1/2 cup ice
½ tsp sea salt

Nutrition
Calories 51
Carbs 5
Fat 4
Protein 2
Sodium 57
Sugar 2

Pecan Coffee Smoothie

Serves: 2
Prep Time: 10 min

Your morning coffee doesn't have to be just a hot dose of caffeine; it can also do double-duty as a flavor base for a delicious smoothie that includes protein-heavy pecans and flaxseed. The tablespoon of maple syrup can be eliminated if you enjoy your coffee sans sugar.

Ingredients
1/2 cup pecans
1/ 2 cup brewed coffee
2 tbsp. flaxseed powder
3/4 cup coconut milk
1/2 cup ice
1 tbsp. maple syrup

Directions
1. Place pecans in blender and crush.
2. Add remaining ingredients and mix until well blended.

Nutrition
Calories 246
Carbs 16
Fat 20
Protein 6
Sodium 8
Sugar 10

Blueberry Coconut Smoothie

Serves: 2
Prep Time: 10 min

The name of the game is protein with a kick of antioxidant. The almonds and flaxseed give those essential amino acids while the blueberries are chock full of antioxidants. This beautiful glass of goodness will have you zipping through your morning.

Ingredients
1/2 cup blueberries
10 walnuts
2 tsp flax seeds
1/2 cup coconut milk
1/2 cup ice

Directions
1. Place all ingredients in blender and mix until well-combined.

Nutrition
Calories 148
Carbs 18
Fat16
Protein 3
Sodium 4
Sugar 9

Spinach Raspberry Smoothie

Serves: 2
Prep Time: 10 min.

Ingredients
1 cup spinach
1/2 cup raspberries
1/2 cup ice
1/2 cup coconut milk

Directions:
1. Place ingredients in food processor and mix until smooth.

Nutrition
Calories 42
Carbs 5
Fat 2
Protein 1
Sodium 32
Sugar 5

Apple Cobbler Smoothie

Serves: 2
Prep Time: 10 min.

A smoothie with the deliciousness of oh-so-delicious apple pie, minus all of the sugary, carby stuff that can slow you down and you have the makings of a wonderful breakfast. The walnuts provide a nice essential amino boost and the whole thing is extremely simple to make.

Ingredients
1 Granny Smith apple, peeled and diced
10 walnuts
1 cup coconut milk
½ cup ice
½ tsp cinnamon
1 tsp maple syrup

Direction
1. Place all ingredients in blender and mix until smooth.

Nutrients
Calories 102
Carbs 12
Fat 8
Protein 6
Sodium 73
Sugar 8

Tomato Celery Perk Smoothie

Serves: 2
Prep Time: 10 min.

Smoothies don't have to be sweet as this savory tomato, carrot, celery proves. The red burst of freshness is a great pick me up first things in the morning and the almonds provide some lasting energy.

Ingredients
1/2 cup celery
1/4 cup carrot
1 lemon, juiced
8 almonds, crushed
3/4 cup low-sodium tomato juice
Salt and pepper to taste

Directions
1. Place carrot and celery in blender and emulsify.
2. Add remaining ingredients and mix until well blended.

Nutrition
Calories 69
Carbs 6
Fat 9
Protein 3
Sodium 35
Sugar 4

Raspberry Almond Smoothie

Serves: 2
Prep Time: 5 min

Raspberries are a good source of antioxidants and they are also on the lower end of the fruit sugar scale, making for a very healthy breakfast drink. The almond and flaxseed provide the omega 3 boost.

Ingredients
1/2 cup raspberries
4 tsp flaxseed
8 almonds
1 cup almond milk
1/2 cup ice

Directions
1. Place ingredients in food processor and blend until combined.

Nutrition
Calories 51
Carbs 5
Fat 4
Protein 2
Sodium 57
Sugar 2

Hawaiian Weekend Smoothie

Serves: 2
Prep Time: 10 min.

This is a tropical weekend smoothie as it brings the flavors of the Caribbean to the breakfast table. Pineapple is combined with coconut milk and the walnuts provide the protein source and add some robustness to the flavor.

Ingredients
1/2 cup pineapple
10 walnuts
1 cup coconut milk
½ cup ice

Directions
1. Place almonds in food processor and chop.
2. Add remaining ingredients and combine well.

Nutrition
Calories 38
Carbs 4
Fat 14
Protein 5
Sodium 75
Sugar 15

Super Green Smoothie

Serves: 2
Prep Time: 10 min.

Go green or go home! This green glass of goodness is chock full of vitamins and minerals with powerful kale and spinach joining forces to provide a breakfast boost that will make for a productive day.

Ingredients
1/2 cup spinach
1/4 cup kale,
1/4 cup green apple
8 almonds
1/2 cup almond milk
1/ 2 cup ice

Directions
1. Place ingredients in blender and mix until well combined.

Nutrition
Calories 37
Carbs 8
Fat 9
Protein 4
Sodium 15
Sugar 3

Lemon Coconut Smoothie

Serves: 2
Prep Time: 10 min.

Lemon is a choice fruit for the Paleo lifestyle as it has one of the lowest amounts of sugar in the fruit family. Amongst a host of health benefits, the lemon zing provides the perfect refreshing start to the day.

Ingredients
8 pecans
1/2 cup fresh lemon juice
1/2 cup coconut milk
1 cup ice
1 tbsp. agave nectar

Directions
1. Place items in food processor and blend until smooth.

Nutrition
Calories 218
Carbs 8
Fat 8
Protein 6
Sodium 16
Sugar 2

Carrot Cashew Smoothie

Serves: 2
Prep Time: 10 min.

Cashew and Carrot make a delicious combination and when combined are a great sources of protein and vitamins. The sprinkling of cardamom powder can take this healthy breakfast smoothie all the way to a lovely dessert.

Ingredients
1/ 2 cup grated carrot
2 tbsp. cashew butter
1 cup coconut milk
1/2 cup ice
1/ 2 tsp cardamom
1 tbsp. maple syrup

Ingredients
1. Place ingredients in blender and mix until smooth.

Nutrition
Calories 127
Carbs 13
Fat 8
Protein 4
Sodium 19
Sugar 7

Orange Vanilla Smoothie

Serves: 2
Prep Time: 5 min.

Mix a little Vitamin C with a little protein power and that is a smoothie that can go from summer to winter and from morning to afternoon.

Ingredients
1/2 cup orange
8 almonds
3 tsp flaxseed
3/4 cup unsweetened vanilla almond milk
1/2 cup ice
1 tsp maple syrup (optional)

Nutrition
Calories 82
Carbs 7
Fat 8
Protein 4
Sodium 57
Sugar 2

Conclusion

One of the biggest benefits of the Paleo lifestyle is the increase in energy many people say they feel. The recipes in this breakfast book are perfect examples of energy-boosting meals that stay true to the Paleo lifestyle and keep you balanced throughout the morning.

These meals also ensure you aren't hankering for some sort of grain by 10 a.m. as the dishes have been planned to keep you full, focused and feeling happy. Having breakfast is an important element of the Paleo lifestyle and by the time you've gone through these 30 days' worth of recipes you will never miss breakfast again as they are so simple and so good.

CPSIA information can be obtained at www.ICGtesting.com
Printed in the USA
LVOW05s1348230214

374814LV00008B/511/P